D0574422

6 2020

NO LONGER PROPERTY OF
SEATTLE PUBLIC LIBRARY

FREE FOR YOU AND ME

WHAT OUR FIRST AMENDMENT MEANS

Christy Mihaly

illustrated by **Manu Montoya**

Albert Whitman & Company
Chicago, Illinois

Our country's *free*.
What does that mean...
for you and me?

Let's go back to when the United States was first created…

We declared our independence
from the far-off British throne.
For ourselves and our descendants,
we would write laws of our own.

And so we wrote the Constitution,
forming a new government,
with rules for every institution—
Congress, courts, and president.

This document would rule the nation,
but there was still more work to do.
Then we had the inspiration
to add a list of freedoms too.

The First Amendment's five protections
guard free speech, free press, and more.
Our liberty to state objections
helps democracy endure.

FREEDOM OF RELIGION

The Constitution makes this clear:
every faith is welcome here.
There's not just *one* our laws protect,
for all alike deserve respect.

When President George Washington visited Newport, Rhode Island, in 1790, the people of the Jewish synagogue there had a question for him.

Mr. President, under this new United States Constitution, will our religion be protected?
Yes, of course! You're welcome here no matter what religion you follow.
The Government of the United States, which gives to bigotry no sanction, to persecution no assistance, requires only that they who live under its protection should [conduct] themselves as good citizens.

This means that each of us can pray
and celebrate in our own way.

FREEDOM OF SPEECH

Because no one is always right,
our founders wisely stated:
"We'll make sure everyone can speak,
so thoughts can be debated."

The First Amendment says that you
can share your point of view—
agree or disagree, discuss,
say what you think is true.

And if we listen carefully
to one side then the other,
we'll have the chance to understand
and learn from one another.

FREEDOM OF THE PRESS

In a democracy, people need news—
facts to consider when forming their views.

That's why reporters keep track of events,
asking hard questions to help things make sense.

They tell us the facts of the world, on our screens and on podcasts, in papers and news magazines.

Knowledge is power; free press is the key—
we must know the truth if we want to stay free.

Look! This newspaper story says the mayor is planning to close our playground... and he wasn't going to tell anyone!

Oh no! That's terrible!

I'm glad that reporter found out the truth!

And then she wrote it in her newspaper story.

FREEDOM OF ASSEMBLY

Freedom of assembly
means Americans can show—
with marches and with rallies—
what they want the world to know.

Let's have a demonstration!
We'll gather those who care,

to sing, parade, and protest,
and make others more aware.

FREEDOM TO PETITION THE GOVERNMENT FOR REDRESS OF GRIEVANCES

When we want to tell our leaders that they're doing something wrong,
we can bring them a petition, and they'll hear our voices, strong.

Politicians need to hear us; we're the ones they represent.
Our leaders keep their jobs only if we give consent.

The freedom of religion,
of speech, and of the press,
the right to peaceful meetings,
the right to seek redress—

these five important freedoms
are democracy's foundation.
Know these rights—defend them—
and we'll build a stronger nation.

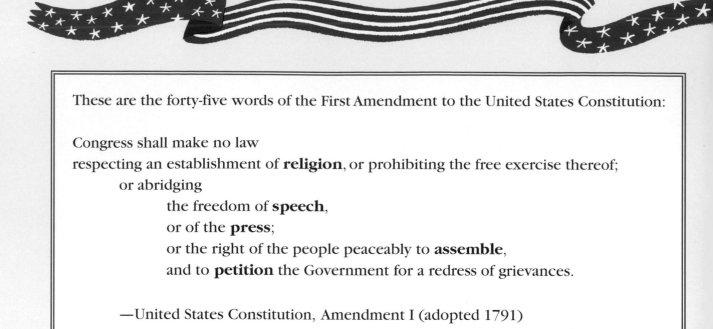

These are the forty-five words of the First Amendment to the United States Constitution:

Congress shall make no law
respecting an establishment of **religion**, or prohibiting the free exercise thereof;
or abridging
the freedom of **speech**,
or of the **press**;
or the right of the people peaceably to **assemble**,
and to **petition** the Government for a redress of grievances.

—United States Constitution, Amendment I (adopted 1791)

ABOUT THE FIRST AMENDMENT

We know the United States is a free country. But many of us—kids and adults alike—aren't always sure what that means. I wrote this book about the First Amendment because it enshrines five of the most fundamental American freedoms.

THE U.S. CONSTITUTION

The thirteen colonies won their independence from Britain in 1783. But it took a few years for the independent states to develop a new system to govern themselves. In the summer of 1787, representatives of the states met in Philadelphia to hammer out rules for a new national government. During that hot summer, with the windows closed so they wouldn't be overheard—and no air conditioning—the delegates debated and worked out their disagreements and disputes. The result was the US Constitution.

The Constitution became the supreme law of the land. But many Americans thought this important document should be more clear about protecting their personal freedoms. In 1791 the first ten amendments—together called the Bill of Rights—were added to the Constitution. In addition to the First Amendment, Bill of Rights provisions include the right to bear arms (Second Amendment), the right to trial by jury (Sixth Amendment), and the prohibition against cruel and unusual punishment (Eighth Amendment). Since then, other important amendments have been added, including the Thirteenth Amendment, abolishing slavery, and the Nineteenth, giving women the right to vote. The most recent amendment, the Twenty-Seventh, was added in 1992.

WHAT DOES THE FIRST AMENDMENT DO?

The First Amendment protects people's rights to self-expression. We express ourselves through what we say, write, create, and do, including our religious practices. The First Amendment also means Americans can tell their government what they think through peaceful protests and petitions. And it says journalists—the press—can investigate and report freely on issues and events people care about. In countries that aren't free, governments may stop the people from doing these things.

One thing to remember: if people don't like what you say, you may have to deal with their reactions. Because they too have the right to free speech.

FREEDOM OF RELIGION
(AND GEORGE WASHINGTON'S LETTER)

The First Amendment says people are free to practice any religion, or no religion. And the government cannot designate any "official" religion or favor one religion over others. This separation of church and state is important to assure that we treat people of all religions fairly.

When the United States was founded, some religions were prohibited in certain countries, and some governments treated people badly if they did not follow their ruler's official religion. Many people sailed to the colonies from Europe in order to freely practice their own faiths.

In 1790, President George Washington visited Newport, Rhode Island, to urge the people there to support the proposed First Amendment. The committee that greeted the president included a representative of the local Jewish synagogue, who read a welcoming letter. A few days later, on August 21, 1790, Washington sent a letter answering the synagogue, confirming that everyone is entitled to religious freedom.

FREEDOM OF SPEECH
(AND THE TRIAL OF MATTHEW LYON)

The First Amendment says the government can't stop people from expressing their opinions. In Britain at this time, people could be arrested for criticizing the king. In the early days of the United States, Americans were still figuring out how much freedom of speech they wanted people to have.

In 1798, the Federalists (John Adams's party) who controlled Congress passed the Sedition Act. *Sedition* means encouraging people to rebel against the government. The new law made it a crime to make "false, scandalous, and malicious" statements about Adams and the Federalist government.

Congressman Matthew Lyon opposed Adams and the Federalist Party. He supported Thomas Jefferson and the Democratic-Republicans. He believed he had a right to criticize the government.

Lyon was arrested and found guilty of criticizing the president. From his chilly,

smelly, uncomfortable jail cell, Lyon ran for reelection. The voters considered Lyon a free speech hero, and they reelected him.

In the 1800 presidential election, Jefferson defeated Adams. In his inaugural address, Jefferson called for unity and emphasized that the First Amendment protects Americans who speak out. He pardoned those who had been convicted under the Sedition Act.

FREEDOM OF THE PRESS

When the First Amendment guaranteed freedom to "the press," it meant to protect newspapers, which were the main source of news in the eighteenth century. Now we get news from radios, television, websites, social media, and more. Freedom of the press means that journalists from all these news media can investigate and report on matters of public interest. Americans can publish information and opinions without government interference.

FREEDOM OF ASSEMBLY AND PETITION

Americans can tell their leaders what they want the government to do. The people have the right to use public protests and petitions to rally supporters and influence government policies. The First Amendment also gives us freedom of association, which includes the right to join organizations without undue government interference. Some historical examples of Americans exercising these rights include:

- **1913:** Seeking women's right to vote, Inez Milholland led a procession on a white horse, wearing a crown and long white cape.

- **1963:** More than 200,000 people gathered for the March on Washington for Jobs and Freedom, and heard Martin Luther King Jr. deliver a speech declaring, "I have a dream."

- **1966:** Thousands of farmworkers and their supporters walked more than 300 miles from Delano, California, to the capitol in Sacramento, calling for better pay and working conditions.

- **2009:** In Tax Day rallies, people protested government spending and demanded lower taxes.

- **2015:** People gathered at public celebrations of the US Supreme Court ruling that same-sex couples had the right to marry.

- **2017:** The Women's March attracted hundreds of thousands of marchers supporting human rights, health care, the environment, science, and other causes.

GLOSSARY

amendment: a change or addition to the Constitution (or other law).

assembly: a meeting or gathering of many people.

US Constitution: the document containing the basic laws of the United States, saying how the government is organized, and guaranteeing the rights of the people.

democracy: a system of government in which voters elect people to represent them and run the government.

faith: a religion.

founders: the people who worked to form the government of the United States, including George Washington, Thomas Jefferson, Alexander Hamilton, and John Adams, among others; sometimes called the Founding Fathers.

grievance: a reason to complain, or a problem such as unfair treatment.

petition: a formal request, often in writing with many signatures.

redress: a way to fix something or make it right.

religion: a system of beliefs and worship of God or gods.

FURTHER READING

THE CONSTITUTION AND BILL OF RIGHTS ONLINE

Original documents and transcripts: https://www.archives.gov/founding-docs/constitution

Text with explanations: https://www.law.cornell.edu/constitution

WEBSITES

Ben's Guide to the US Government: https://bensguide.gpo.gov/

iCivics, civics learning and games: https://www.icivics.org/

BOOKS FOR YOUNG READERS

Flags Over America: A Star-Spangled Story by Cheryl Harness. Albert Whitman, 2014.

The Bill of Rights: Protecting Our Freedom Then and Now by Syl Sobel. Barron's Educational Series, 2008.

We the People: The Constitution of the United States of America by Peter Spier. Doubleday Books for Young Readers, 2014.

Today on Election Day by Catherine Stier, illustrated by David Leonard. Albert Whitman, 2012.

To Erzsi, for her belief in the First Amendment and in me.
CM

To my family
MM

Library of Congress Cataloging-in-Publication data is on file with the publisher.

Text copyright © 2020 by Christy Mihaly
Illustrations copyright © 2020 by Albert Whitman & Company
Illustrations by Manu Montoya
First published in the United States of America in 2020 by Albert Whitman & Company
ISBN 978-0-8075-2441-1 (hardcover)
ISBN 978-0-8075-2445-9 (e-book)

All rights reserved. No part of this book may be reproduced or transmitted in any
form or by any means, electronic or mechanical, including photocopying,
recording, or by any information storage and retrieval system,
without permission in writing from the publisher.

Printed in China
10 9 8 7 6 5 4 3 2 1 WKT 24 23 22 21 20 19

Design by Rick DeMonico

For more information about Albert Whitman & Company,
visit our website at www.albertwhitman.com.

★ ★ ★ ★ ★ ★ ★ ★

★ ★ ★ ★ ★ ★ ★ ★

★ ★ ★ ★ ★ ★ ★ ★

★ ★ ★ ★ ★ ★ ★ ★

★ ★ ★ ★ ★ ★ ★ ★

★ ★ ★ ★ ★ ★ ★ ★

★ ★ ★ ★ ★ ★ ★ ★

★ ★ ★ ★ ★ ★ ★ ★